Sow to the Spirit
A Study of the Book of Galatians

Beth Bingaman

For the one who sows to his own flesh will from the flesh reap corruption, but the one who sows to the Spirit will from the Spirit reap eternal life.
Galatians 6:8

ISBN – 13: 978-1726030892
* Scripture quotations are from The Holy Bible, English Standard Version® (ESV®), copyright © 2001 by Crossway, a publishing ministry of Good News Publishers. Used by permission. All rights reserved.

Table of Contents

Sow to the Spirit:
A Study of the Book of Galatians

6 Week Study

Introduction

Sow to the Spirit:
A Study of the Book of Galatians
Written by Beth Bingaman

...but the one who sows to the Spirit will from the Spirit reap eternal life. Galatians 6:8b

As Christians, we see the need to discern between "scriptural teaching" and "false teaching" so that we are not distracted from efforts to build the Kingdom of God.

"Legalism" is the term we have given the teaching that the Galatians encountered. It is something we must learn to avoid so our works will be fruitful. It is the core of the matter that concerned Paul in this letter.

Scholars differ on exactly when Paul wrote the letter, most agree it was between A.D. 49-55. There is less agreement on which Galatians to whom it was written (Celtic Galatians that lived in the North or Galatian churches). What does seem certain is that they were people of Galatia who were believers in the Lord Jesus Christ. Paul addresses the letter "To the churches in Galatia."

False teachers came in after these believers had placed their faith in Christ and Paul had travelled on to continue his ministry to others. These agitators were adding to the Gospel that Paul presented to them, insisting that the Galatians must be circumcised to be saved.

Paul teaches them that it is faith alone that justifies them before God, not human merit for obeying laws like circumcision. He warns them that the one who "sows to please his sinful nature, from that nature will reap destruction; the one who sows to please the Spirit, from the Spirit will reap eternal life" Galatians 6:8).

The parallels to our own day are evident as we study. The agitators show pride in their own traditions and ideas about what God requires while ignoring the scriptures. (See Galatians 2:3-5, 5:2, 6, 11; 6:12-13, 15). They also malign Paul personally, taking aim at his integrity and attempting to separate them from him and his teaching (Galatians 4:16-17).

In his closing chapters, Paul encourages the Galatian believers with the fruits of the Spirit (Chapter 5). Further, he reminds them that they are free in Christ (chapter 6). He is clear that this is not freedom to sin, but freedom to live in obedience and blessing as they rely on the Holy Spirit.

Through this study you will learn the importance of discerning between the false teacher and the true teacher. It is also vital for us to learn to live according to the Spirit and not the flesh. Through the Holy Spirit, God used Paul to exhort the Galatians and us. The book has been preserved for our good and His glory.

Using this Study Guide

The purpose of this study guide is to help you keep your mind on the passages as you work through each chapter. Paul has written a convicting letter. The questions walk you through what he is teaching so that as you study you will see the applications to your life today.

Each time you sit down to study you will want to begin with prayer. Ask the Holy Spirit to teach you as you go through each question. Gathering with a group to discuss the answers after you have completed the lessons will help you to fully develop your thoughts and hear how God is working in others through the study of His Word.

I pray that each one who uses the book will grow in faith, knowledge and understanding of God's Word, for His glory and the advancement of His Kingdom.

Galatians 1

Read Galatians 1:1-5

1. Paul is writing to rebuke the Galatians for allowing false teachers to come to them and add to the gospel Paul had given them when he had been with them. They have added ceremonies to the truth Paul had taught them of salvation through faith. How does Paul present the Gospel in these first 5 verses?

2. Read Acts 9:1-7 and Acts 13:2-3. Why does Paul assert in Galatians 1:1 that he is not called by men, but by God?

3. Why does Paul greet the Galatians and offer them, "Grace and peace to you from God our Father and the Lord Jesus Christ"? (If they have grace and peace, what does that mean for them?)

4. In Galatians 1:4, Paul indicates that this grace includes that Christ gave Himself for our sins to deliver us.

A. Why do you think Paul reminds them so soon in the letter?

B. What do you think Paul is communicating with the words, "according to the will of our God and Father"?

Read Galatians 1:6-14

5. How do we see the gospel of Christ perverted by false teachers today?

6. We have heard it said that we need to be reminded of the truths of the gospel of Christ every day. How does this passage support or refute that statement?

7. Read Galatians 1:9-10. Paul asserts that he is purposefully serving God and not man. Examine your own thoughts, words, and works. What are you doing that serves your own, or another person's interests over God's purposes (i.e, fear, lies, gossip, complacency, sloth)?

8. Is it possible, according to Paul, to serve both God and men? How do we justify this with the command to serve one another?

9. Paul describes receiving the gospel through the revelation of Jesus Christ. What means did God use to introduce you to the person of Jesus Christ and the truth of the gospel?

Read Galatians 1:15-24

10. From Galatians 1:11-21, list the steps Paul gives for the Galatians to see how God has directed him after his conversion.

11. "But he who set me apart before I was born" (Galatians 1:17). Explain this statement in your own words (See also Jeremiah 1:5; Isaiah 49:1; Romans 8:30, Ephesians 1:4).

12. If someone were to malign the character of Paul, calling him a fraud, how would you refute their claims? Can you describe the revelation given to him by Christ on the road to Damascus in Acts 9?

13. Looking at Galatians 1:22-24, what changes have others seen in you that might cause them to glorify God? How does the way you live and speak honor or glorify God?

Outside the Box: How would we recognize someone who comes into the church and "distorts the gospel of Christ?" What course of action should we take with such a person?

Galatians 2

Questions for Discussion

Read Galatians 2:1-5

1. In Galatians 2:1-2 Paul makes a trip back to Jerusalem. How can we imitate the course of action he took to check on the accuracy of the doctrine he was teaching?

2. What is the significance of the fact that those they spoke to did not insist that Titus be circumcised?

3. Galatians 2:4 says, "Yet because of false brothers secretly brought in--who slipped in to spy out our freedom that we have in Christ Jesus, so that they might bring us into slavery..." What liberty is Paul talking about? What slavery does he refer to?

Read Galatians 2:6-10

4. Compare Paul's words regarding the Apostles in Galatians 2:6 with his comment about them (and himself) in 1 Corinthians 15:9.

5. From Galatians 2:7. Are these distinctions of their calls (Paul to the uncircumcised and Cephas (Peter) to the circumcised) hard lines, not to be crossed?

6. What "grace" was perceived to have been given to Paul and what is understood by James, Cephas, and John, "extending the right hand of fellowship" to him?

7. Why did they all agree that Paul and Barnabas should "remember the poor" to the Gentiles? (See Romans 15:27)

Read Galatians 2:11-16

8. What authority does Paul have to correct Peter?

9. Why do you think he rebuked him publicly? Is there a principle here that applies to us? If so, how?

10. Does God have different expectations for Jews and Gentiles? If so, what are they? (See Romans 4:2-8 and 10:4)

11. Romans 3:20 says, "For by works of the law no human being will be justified in his sight, since through the law comes knowledge of sin." What is one purpose of the law, according to this verse?

Read Galatians 2:17-21

12. Read Galatians 2:17-19 and Romans 7:4-7. Paul, turning from Cephas back to the Galatians, confirms the truth of his teaching regarding Christ's sacrifice and the ceremonial laws (that the false teachers were introducing). How does Romans 7:4-7 clarify Paul's message of salvation by faith and the value of God's law?

13. What had Paul "torn down" (verse 18) that he did not want to rebuild? In what ways are we (or our churches) tearing down what has been built by/for us?

14. From Galatians 2:20, how do Christians "live by faith?"

15. What does Paul mean, "if righteousness were through the law, then Christ died for no reason?"

Outside the Box: We are only in chapter 2 and Paul has used the word "grace" 5 times. One of the false teachings of our day is that the God of the New Testament is the God of grace, suggesting that God was not gracious in the Old Testament. The Bible says that God is the same yesterday, today, and forever. How did God demonstrate His grace in the Old Testament?

Galatians 3

Questions for Discussion

Read Galatians 3:1-5

Note: Galatians 3:1 gives us Paul's argument that his teaching about Christ's crucifixion was as clear as if he had painted a picture for them. It is as if the Galatians had actually seen the life and death of Christ through the teaching of Paul.[i]

Personal: What do you need to do to be prepared to paint such a word picture of Christ's life and death? (See 1 Corinthians 2:2-5)

1. In Galatians 3:2 Paul asks the Galatians to remember the work of the Holy Spirit that brought them to faith. How can we apply this question to our own lives when we are tempted to stray from the sound doctrine we have been taught?

Note: In his commentary, John Calvin suggests that Paul's asking, "Who has bewitched you?" is indicative that the Galatians have fallen for a supernatural deception of Satan. He points out that it is not that the Galatians did not believe the truth when they heard it, but that they had failed to persevere in obedience. [ii]

2. This resulted in Paul's question in Galatians 3:3, "Are you so foolish? Having begun by the Spirit, are you now being perfected by the flesh?" Who is Paul referring to by "Spirit," and as "flesh?"

3. In verse 5, Paul switches his emphasis to what God has done among the Galatians (given His Spirit and performed miracles to bring them to faith) from which the false teachers were directing them away.   What false doctrines have been introduced today that have the same goal?

4. Read Galatians 3:6-9 (with Psalm 37:39, 149:4; Habakkuk 2:4; Romans 3:23-24, 28, 4:2-5; Hebrews 10:37-39). Considering all of these verses, what is the point Paul is continuing to make to the Galatians (and us)? Why is this so important?

Read Galatians 3:10-14

5. Paul teaches that everyone is cursed by the Law because they do not abide by the Law (Galatians 3:10), and further that no one is ever justified by the Law. Remembering his purpose in writing to the Galatians, what point is Paul continuing to make?

6. In Romans 10:9 Paul says, "because, if you confess with your mouth that Jesus is Lord and believe in your heart that God raised him from the dead, you will be saved." Considering Matthew 5:17, John 14:15 and James 2:8, does the faith Paul describes in Romans 10:9 eliminate our need to keep God's Law?

7. What is the truth revealed in Galatians 3:13-14?

Read Galatians 3:15-18

8. There are two schools of thought regarding God's covenants. In scripture we find the Adamic (Genesis 3:14-19); Noahic (Genesis 9:15-17); Abrahamic (Genesis 17:19-21); Davidic (2 Samuel 7:12-17); and the New Covenant in Christ, (Ezekiel 36:26-27, Hebrews 8:6-10). The first school of thought believes that each new covenant nullifies the older one. The second believes that each new covenant builds upon the older ones. According to Galatians 3:15-18, which school of thought is Paul teaching? Why is this important?

9. What are the promises of the New Covenant? (See Jeremiah 31:31-34; Ezekiel 36:26-27; Hebrews 8:6-10; Luke 22:19-20; 2 Corinthians 3:5-6)

Read Galatians 3:19-29

10. "Why then the Law?" How does Paul answer this question? (see Romans 2:13, 3:19-20, 7:7)

11. A. How would our own culture be different if the Ten Commandments were the laws of the state?

B. Why should Christians be willing to proclaim/teach God's Law to everyone?

12. John Calvin teaches that "the intermediary" who "put the promise in place"[iii] in Galatians 3:19-20, is Jesus Christ. Paul says that, though the promise was originally given to the Jews, the Gentiles are now included. (See Ephesians 2:11-13) One Mediator, one God, gives His promise to both Jews and Gentiles. Considering what we know of what the false teachers were saying about the need to keep the ceremonial laws, why is Paul giving the Galatians (and us) this information?

13. In Galatians 3:22-26 Paul points out the result of keeping the Law and faith in Christ. Summarize his teaching in your own words.

14. In the ESV, Galatians 3:23 says, "Now before faith came, we were held captive under the law, imprisoned until the coming faith would be revealed." (We acknowledge here that there was a measure of faith that we have already seen, Abraham was counted righteous because of it.) John Calvin suggests this phrase "before faith came" is a comparison to what God revealed as faith in the New Testament. What is the nature of this "captivity" according to Galatians 4:4-5, 5:18; Hebrews 11:13?

15. As the "guardian" (ESV) or schoolmaster (KJV), what was the job of God's Law?

16. Read 2 Timothy 3:16-17 and comment on how we should view the Law of God today.

17. Read Galatians 3:27; Job 29:14; Isaiah 61:10; and Colossians 3:10. Explain what it means to "put on Christ."

18. In this letter, Paul repeatedly makes the point of teaching that justification is by faith (Galatians 3:24). Take a moment to remember who he is teaching and why. With this in mind, what is his message in Galatians 3:28-29? (Paul keeps making this point so there must be a reason he wants to repeat it. So, if it feels like you have already answered this question, you are right.)

19. The Jews believed their greatest distinction was that they were the "offspring of Abraham," and therefore the "sons of God." Who does Paul include as "Abraham's offspring" and why? (See Romans 4:9, 12, 16, 9:7-8)

Outside the Box: Romans 9:6-8 say, "But it is not as though the Word of God has failed. For not all who are descended from Israel belong to Israel, and not all are children of Abraham because they are his offspring, but 'Through Isaac shall your offspring be named.' This means it is not the children of the flesh who are the children of God, but the children of the promise (Genesis 17:21) are counted as offspring." In light of what Paul is trying to turn the Galatians away from with regard to the teaching that had come into the Galatian church, why is what he teaches in Romans 9:6-8 important?

Galatians 4

Questions for Discussion

Paul is continuing his teaching that the law is a "guardian" or "schoolmaster." John Calvin explains Galatians 4:1: "The elect, though they are children of God from the womb, yet, until by faith they come to the possession of freedom, remain like slaves under the law; but, from the time that they have known Christ, they no longer require this kind of tutelage."[iv]

Read Galatians 4:1-5

1. In Galatians 4:1-2 Paul compares the "children of God" with slaves who are under the authority of their masters, the law being the "guardian and manager (ESV)" of God's people though they are heirs (owners of everything) until the date set by the father. How is it that, even today, we, as heirs, await the date set by the father to fully experience and understand our inheritance and adoption?

Note: "Elementary principles of the world" (Galatians 4:3) are defined by Matthew Henry as "being tied to a great number of burdensome rites and observances, by which, as by a kind of first rudiments they were taught and instructed, and whereby they were kept in a state of subjection, like a child under the tutors and governors."[v]

2. The "elementary principles of the world" (ESV) were spiritually significant. Why does Paul say they are "of the world"?

3. How are people (Christian and/or non-Christian) today living as though God's laws are "elementary principles of the world?"

4. What does the phrase, "when the fullness of time had come," indicate about God sending Jesus Christ for our redemption?

5. In Galatians 4:4 Paul says, "God sent forth His Son," and that He was "born of a woman." What two truths about Christ do these confirm?

6. What is the significance of Jesus being "born under the law," as those He redeems are "under the law?"

7. How is the Trinity revealed in Galatians 4:4-6?

Read Galatians 4:4-12

8. What is Paul describing in Galatians 4:4-7?

9. Read Galatians 4:6 with Ephesians 1:13-14, and 2 Corinthians 5:5. What truth of our salvation is confirmed in these verses?

10. According to John 14:26, Acts 1:8, Romans 5:5, 15:13, and 2 Timothy 1:14, what does the Christian receive with the gift of the Holy Spirit?

11. **Personal**: "Crying, Abba Father." (Galatians 4:6). The word "crying" is apparently not describing "tears of sorrow" but "boldly proclaiming." Reflecting on your own faith, are you taking every opportunity to "boldly proclaim the name of "Abba Father"? If not, why not?

12. What distinction does Paul make between a slave and a son? (See Galatians 4:7)

13. In Galatians 4:8-9, Paul reminds the Galatians that before God revealed Himself to them, they were enslaved by idols ("gods that are not gods").
A. What "worthless elementary principles (4:9) of the world" does he specifically name in verse 10?

B. Why does this make him feel as if he has labored in vain (Galatians 4:11)?

Read Galatians 4:12-20 (Notice that Paul softens his tone.)

14. Read 2 Timothy 4:2. How does Paul practice what he preaches in Galatians 4:12-20?

15. John Calvin suggests that Paul says, "You did me no wrong," to remind the Galatians that his words are not out of anger or revenge.[vi] Why then, should they suppose that Paul has used strong language with them up to this point?

16. In Galatians 4:16, Paul asks, "Have I then become your enemy by telling you the truth?" Is sharing the truth of scripture with someone an act of love or enmity? Why?

17. Most Christians remember the joy and blessedness they felt when God opened their eyes and ears to the truth, giving them faith. How would you answer Paul's question, "What then has become of your blessedness (Galatians 4:15)?"

18. In Galatians 4:17-18, Paul seems to be calling the Galatians to have the same love for him when he is absent as they showed him when he was with them. How real is zeal for the truth that fades when the instructor has gone away? How do we see the same thing today?

Note: Verse 19 starts, "My little children," soft and affectionate, though Paul may also be reminding them that they should not still be "little children." He says that he is enduring anguish as if he were in childbirth, that they might have Christ formed in them. Paul compares himself to a woman in labor as if to say that the Galatians are not yet fully born.

19. In Galatians 4:12 Paul entreats them, "Become as I am." In verse 19 he tells them he is in anguish of childbirth until Christ is formed in you." What does Paul want for the Galatians (and us)?

Read Galatians 4:21-31

20. Paul sets up Abraham's two sons as an allegory. One son was born of a slave woman and one was born of a free woman. Ishmael is the son of the slave woman, and Isaac is the son of the free woman. List what you learn about each.

Slave:	Free:

21. In Galatians 4:25 Paul says that Hagar is Mt. Sinai in Arabia and that she corresponds to the present day Jerusalem. What do you think Mt. Sinai and Jerusalem had in common in Paul's day?

22. "But the Jerusalem above is free and she is our mother." (Galatians 4:26) John Calvin explains that this Jerusalem is not to be looked for "in" heaven or out of this world. He says, "The Church is spread over the whole world and is a stranger and pilgrim on the earth."[vii]   If Calvin is right, this is not referring to actual heaven but to God's universal church on earth. What freedoms do those who are in God's universal Church experience today? (See also Isaiah 52:9, 66:10-14; Micah 4:1-2; 2 Corinthians 3:17; John 8:34-36; and Romans 6:7.)

23. The passage Paul quotes in Galatians 4:27 (from Isaiah 54) refers to the call of the Gentiles and promises barren women and widows numerous offspring. In his commentary, John Calvin says that Isaiah proclaims that these children will be called from all nations of the earth, not because of anything the barren woman does but, by "the grace and blessing of God (Isaiah 54:1-8)."[viii]   What is the main point of Paul's teaching in Galatians 4: 26-28?

24. Read Galatians 4:29 with Genesis 21:8-9 (you may also refer to Matthew 23:34-37 and 1 Thessalonians 2:14-15). What comparison is Paul making in Galatians 4:29?

Outside the box: Read Genesis 21:8-12
As harsh as it sounds to us, how do we know that Sarah was not wrong to ask for Hagar and Ishmael to be sent away?

25. Galatians 4:31 says, "So, brothers, we are not children of the slave but of the free woman." What significance does this verse have for Christians today?

Galatians 5

Questions for Discussion

Paul is continuing in his arguments against the false teachers. In Galatians 5:1 Paul says, "For freedom Christ has set us free; stand firm therefore, and do not submit again to a yoke of slavery." John Calvin explains in his commentary that this freedom Paul is talking about is the "liberty we have in the exemption from the ceremonies of the law, the observance of which was demanded by the false apostles as necessary."[ix]
Keep in mind as we continue through this book that the Galatians were not Jews. They had never practiced the ceremonial laws of God.

Read Galatians 5:1-6

1. Calvin says, "This liberty was processed for us by Christ, on the cross: the fruit and possession of it are bestowed upon us through the Gospel."[x]

A. Explain:

B. What warning does Paul give Christians in Galatians 5:3-6?

Note: From Calvin's commentary on Galatians 5:3: "A very striking example occurs in this passage. When Abraham had received a promise concerning Christ, and justification by free grace, and eternal salvation, circumcision was added, in order to confirm the promise; and thus it became, by the appointment of God, a sacrament, which was subservient to faith. Next come false apostles, who pretend that it is a meritorious work, and recommend the observance of the law, making a profession of obedience to it to be signified by circumcision as an initiatory rite. Paul makes reference here to the appointment of God, but attacks the unscriptural views of the false apostles."[xi]

2. Are there similar examples today where a ceremony is given more weight or effect than God has given it?

3. Read Acts 16:1-5. Why does Paul circumcise Timothy?

4. What should our own attitude be as we participate in God's sacraments of Baptism and the Lord's Supper?

5. From Galatians 5:5, where does Paul place our "hope of righteousness?"

6. In Galatians 5:6, Paul says the only thing that counts for anything is, "faith working through love." What is Paul saying about the connection between faith, love, and works?

Read Galatians 5:7-12

7. In Galatians 5:7, Paul apparently wants to cause the Galatians to feel ashamed of believing the false teachers. In verse 8 he assures them that what they are doing is not from God. In verse 9, he warns them that this false doctrine could spread like leaven through a lump of dough. In our culture it is considered politically incorrect to try to induce guilt or shame in others.

A. Why is Paul unafraid to speak so boldly?

B. Is it a good tactic for today? Why or why not?

Read Galatians 5:10-12

8. Paul clearly faults the false teachers.

A. What is he confident God will do?

B. In Galatians 5:11, what does Paul mean by the "offense of the cross?"

C. What does he pray the false teachers will do? Is this surprising? Why?

D. Is the glory of God more important than the salvation of men?

9. Read John 10:11-13. What do these verses say about the "Shepherd" who allows false teachers access to his flock?

Read Galatians 5:13-18

10. Paul reminds the Galatians of their freedom in Christ but begins to explain how it should spill into their relationships with other people (Galatians 5:13-15) What does he say they have the freedom (liberty) to do?

11. How can we "use our freedom to, "through love, serve one another?"

12. How do we love our neighbor as we love ourselves?

13. How does one, "walk by the Spirit?" (see Galatians 5:16-18 and Romans 8:5-11)

14. Paul acknowledges in Galatians 5:17 and Romans 7:15 that we will all be tempted to do things we do not want to do.

A. What is the gracious truth Paul offers us in Galatians 5:18?

B. Why was this a gracious thing to say to the Galatians at the time Paul was writing?

Note: Paul has made the point that all Christians should be walking by the Spirit, not the flesh. He now offers a description of the flesh and then of the Spirit. He was leaving no wiggle room for his hearers.

Read Galatians 5:19-26

15. **Personal**: Examine the list he calls "works of the flesh."

A. Which do you struggle with? Which would your family, friends, or co-workers think you struggle with?

B. In Galatians 5:21 Paul warns that "those who do such things will not inherit the Kingdom of God." Assuming this means a person in whom at least one of these sins is a regular behavior, is your calling and election sure? (See 2 Peter 1:10 and 1 John 3:9)

16. Now examine Paul's list of the fruits of the Spirit in Galatians 5:22-23. Thinking from a long term view (not how you "feel" today), are there any you do not experience? If there is even one, please consider why you might not experience it. Things to consider:

- Am I walking with the Spirit?

- Is there a truth about God that I do not believe (in practice, even if I say I do)?

- Is there a sin I have not confessed?

- Am I obeying God's commands?

- Have I believed any false teaching?

Outside the Box: Looking at Galatians 5:16-24, can you think of similar lessons the Bible teaches regarding "the flesh" and "the Spirit" or sin and righteousness (whether or not it uses the same terms)?

17. Paul closes the chapter with a warning against conceit, provoking one another, and envying one another. How does conceit lead to provoking and/or envying one another? How is this a problem in the Church today?

Galatians 6

Questions for Discussion

Read Galatians 6:1-5

1. Paul teaches that when someone is "caught in any transgression," the spiritual Christian "should restore him in a spirit of gentleness." What godly attributes will be shown in a "spirit of gentleness" and "those who are spiritual?"

2. Galatians 6:1b says, "Keep watch on yourself, lest you too be tempted." What are we watching for so we are not tempted?

Outside the Box: Before confronting another to gently restore a brother or sister in sin, what do we need to do? Are there other verses that address this?

3. "Bear one another's burdens and so fulfill the law of Christ." Galatians 6:2.

A. According to Matthew 22:36-40, what is the law of Christ we are to fulfill by bearing these burdens?

B. What kind of burdens might Paul be referring to as they relate to restoring a brother who is caught in sin?

Read Galatians 6:3-4

Personal: Examine your own faith and works accordingly.

4. In verse 5, Paul points us to the truth that each one of us will bear our own burden. According to Jeremiah 32:19; Ezekiel 18:4; Matthew 16:27; and 2 Corinthians 5:10-11, what does it mean to "bear our own load (ESV)?"

Read Galatians 6:6-10

5. In his commentary, John Calvin teaches that "the teachers and ministers of the Word were at this time neglected."[xii] Read 1 Corinthians 9:11-14 and explain what Paul was teaching Christians.

6. According to 2 Timothy 4:2; Acts 20:27; 2 Corinthians 1:24; and Ephesians 3:7-10, what is the one who is teaching the Word of God responsible to do?

7. "Do not be deceived, God is not mocked (Galatians 6:7). This statement refers back to the proclamation to share all good things with those who teach the Word (Galatians 6:6). It is directed at those who would make excuses for why they cannot give and pointing out that it is God who gets cheated by such excuses.[xiii] He also points out that those who have so little regard for their teachers/preachers that they will not help him with his needs, are showing no regard for God and His Word.

A. **Personal**: How do you show appreciation for those who preach and teach you?

B. Are there other things Christians do (or fail to do) that might not be recognized as mocking God, but do mock Him?

8. Explain the terms, "sow to the flesh" and "sow to the Spirit" from Galatians 6:8.

9. What is Paul admonishing us to do in Galatians 6:9-10? Why is he teaching that?

10. In Galatians 6:10 Paul tells us to take the opportunities given to us to do good to everyone, "and especially those of the household of faith." Why do you think he calls us the "household of faith?"

11. List the attributes of God you find in Galatians 6:1-10.

Read Galatians 6:11-18

12. We use all capital letters to express how loudly we want someone to "hear" out texts. Paul apparently practiced the same principle in expressing his anxiety about the subject matter of his letter to the Galatians. What concern does he express in this last warning in Galatians 12-13?

13. Paul compares the false teachers who "want to make a good showing in the flesh," with himself who would not "boast except in the cross of our Lord Jesus Christ." What do you know of "the cross" in which you can glory?

14. How does Galatians 2:20 help to explain what Paul means by, "by which the world has been crucified to me, and I to the world." (See also Philippians 3:7-11)

15. From Galatians 6:15, what does it mean to be a "new creation?" (See 2 Corinthians 5:17; Ezekiel 36:26)

16. In verse 16 Paul pronounces a blessing of peace and mercy on "those who walk by this rule," (that a new creation is all that counts). John Calvin teaches that this "rule" is the "regular and habitual course which all godly ministers of the gospel ought to pursue." He prays the same blessing upon the "Israel of God." Who is Paul referring to by "the Israel of God?" (See Galatians 3:9; Romans 2:28-29, 9:6-8)

17. In Galatians 6:17, Paul seems to return to his more authoritative tone, "From now on let no one cause me trouble, for I bear on my body the marks of Jesus," reminding them how he has suffered for Jesus Christ.

A. Considering his consistent message in this letter to the Galatians, what do you think he is trying to communicate to them?

B. How does this apply to today's Christian?

The grace of our Lord Jesus Christ be with your spirit, brothers (and sisters). Amen. Galatians 6:18

Galatians 1 Answers

Galatians 1:1-5

1. Verses 4 and 5 teach that Christ gave Himself for our sins – to deliver us from the present evil age (which we are enslaved to by our sin) – according to the will of God, our Father. Verse 1 reminds us Jesus is the Living God, raised from the dead.

2. Paul had direct contact with Jesus on the road to Damascus, His voice was not coming from a man with Paul, but was the supernatural communication of the Living God. In Acts 13 the Holy Spirit confirmed Paul's call to serve the Lord.

3. Grace and peace come from God alone – he is praying for their salvation.

4. A. He may remind them because they are about to be rebuked for forgetting what they knew was true about their sin. They were adding to the Gospel of Christ. Paul is fearful for them about their salvation.

B. He is not speaking with his own authority but is calling on the ultimate Authority, God Himself. And, reminding them that he is their father, too (using the word "our.").

Galatians 1:6-14

5. Personal

6. It reveals how easy it is to listen to people who seem so spiritual yet they are not speaking according to the Word of God. It is a temptation of man to be led astray if we do not keep ourselves grounded in the truth.

7. Personal

8. No, we cannot serve both. Our heart and motives are at the root of this question. We are to serve one another, in the love of Christ, for the sake of the Name of Jesus Christ. "They will know us by our love."

9. Personal

Galatians 1:15-24

10.
- Set apart before birth and called by grace
- God revealed His Son to Paul
- Went to Arabia then to Damascus
- To Jerusalem for 15 days to visit Cephas
- Then to regions of Syria and Cilicia
- Remained unknown to the churches in Judea but they were hearing of him, "that he used to persecute but is now preaching faith he once tried to destroy."

11. God, in the grace of His election, chooses those He will save, predestined them before the foundations of the world. It has always been how He works.

12. Paul had a personal encounter with Jesus Christ on that road to Damascus. The only way to describe it as a supernatural encounter where Jesus identified Himself and miraculously worked to bring Paul to faith. Only God can give someone the eyes to see the truth of this.

13. Personal

Outside the Box:
A false teacher is recognized because their teaching does not line up with scripture. We have to be willing to check all teaching with scripture, go to them and question them to discern their intent, and then go back with someone else if they will not listen and finally take them to the church (Matthew 18) if they refuse to be corrected from the scriptures. The may need to be asked to leave the church if they are not convicted and repentant of their sin.

Galatians 2 Answers

Galatians 2:1-5

1. Paul went back to consult with the most learned and wise men he knew on the scriptures. We can emulate this by being the "Berean" (Acts 17:10-11) and seeking first to check what we hear with scripture. If we still need help, we need to seek out those who have knowledge and understanding of the scriptures so we live and teach sound doctrine.

2. The false teachers had been teaching that new converts had to be circumcised in order to be saved (or to prove one was saved). These learned men Paul consulted did not agree but advised that the non-Jew was free not to follow that tradition if they chose not to.

3. The liberty he talks about is our liberty to not have to continue to do works and keep the law for our salvation. The slavery was all of the ceremonial laws the Jews had to keep for the atonement of sin. Once Christ paid that debt, those sacrifices and ceremonies were no longer required.

Galatians 2:6-10

4. In Galatians 2 Paul is talking about his knowledge of the way of salvation and sound doctrine. The Apostles (influential men) were not able to add to his understanding. In 1 Corinthians 15:9 he was referring to his overall status as "the least of the Apostles" (ESV) because of his past. He had persecuted God's people for a long time before he came to faith.

5. No. Both would minister to anyone but had specific calls.

6. He was truly saved by the grace of God, no longer actively or even willing, to persecute Christians any more.
Their "right hand of fellowship" acknowledged that they saw the changed nature in him.

7. As the gospel was spreading the responsibility to share the wealth among the brothers in need was acknowledged as part of loving their neighbors.

Galatians 2:11-16

8. The same authority as any Christian has with another. Admonish one another. 1 Thessalonians 5:12-14. There may also be a feeling of responsibility as he taught and led some of them to the Lord, 1 Corinthians 4:14

9. Paul rebuked Peter publicly because he was leading people (even Barnabas who should have known better) astray publicly. In order to correct the example with everyone, he had to tell everyone. Principle: When a sin against us is between us and someone else, the rebuke should be quiet and between just two. When the sin affects more, more may need to hear the correction (using discernment regarding the need for this and getting the log out of our own eye first.)

10. No.

11. The law gives us the knowledge of sin.

Galatians 2:17-21

12. He reminds them that we died with Christ – dying to the law (Romans 7:4) in order to bear fruit for God. We left bearing fruit for death when our sinfulness was aroused by the law (wanting to do what we should not do). We live under the new way of the Spirit - not the old way of the law for our salvation.

13. Paul tore down the Old Covenant thinking that we had to perfectly obey the Law and make sacrifices for atonement of sin.

14. Recognizing and yielding to Christ living in us, working through the power of the Holy Spirit, and not trying to act in our own power.

15. Christ was sent to "save us from our sins." He took the punishment of death (The wages of sin is death. Romans 6:23). If we were able to earn our salvation by perfectly keeping the law, then Christ died in vain. Because we cannot keep the law, then we need Him desperately to impute His righteousness to us through faith.

Outside the Box:
God repeatedly showed grace and mercy to the people of Israel. Even in judgment they were offered repeated opportunities to turn back to God before He judged them. In Deuteronomy 11 God promised blessings for obedience and curses for disobedience. When Israel obeyed, God did bless them.

Galatians 3 Answers

Galatians 3:1-5

Personal

1. With a clear knowledge and understanding of the work of the Holy Spirit in us, we can remind ourselves of what we know to be true about Him when we are tempted to stray.

2. The Spirit is the Holy Spirit of God. The flesh is the sinful desires of man.

3. Personal experiences will vary. Some examples: the prosperity gospel, our faith is a strictly personal matter, salvation is in baptism, supporting "Pro-life" legislation as "good" when it still allows for the murder of babies in their mother's womb.

4. It is by faith we are saved, not by works and we have to stick with sound doctrine and not listen to those who do not know Christ. It is important because some false teachers will come into our churches. They may lead some believers astray by not teaching the truth of God's Word.

Galatians 3: 10-14

5. These false teachers are leading them astray by adding "works" to their requirements for salvation.

6. No. We do not need to perfectly keep the law in order to be saved. In this way we are not bound by it. Jesus said that He came to fulfill, not abolish the Law and He says we are to obey His commands. Though no one is righteous by keeping the Law there are blessings for obeying it.

7. That we receive the Spirit through faith in Jesus Christ. He took the curse as our punishment on that tree. He redeemed those who place their faith in Him. Righteousness passes from Christ to us when He gives us faith.

Galatians 3:15-18

8. Paul is teaching that each covenant builds on the others. No promise of God's is ever null and void (fulfilled in some cases, but never rescinded). God is trustworthy and His trustworthiness stands on the inerrancy of His Word.

9. God will put the law within us and write it on our hearts. He will be our God and we will be His people (Jeremiah 31:31-33)
Give us a new heart and a new Spirit. He will remove the heart of stone and replace it with a heart of flesh. He will cause us to walk in His statutes and obey His rules, dwell in the land. (Ezekiel 36)
He will put His laws in our minds and write them on our hearts. He will be our God and we will be His people. They will know Him. He will be merciful of our iniquities and remember our sins no more. (Hebrews 8)
His body and blood have been given for us. (Luke 22)
He has made us ministers of this New Covenant. (1 Corinthians)

Galatians 3:19-29

10. The law reveals sin and righteousness in that God looks for the doers of the Law. Through the Law comes knowledge of sin.

11. Answers will vary.

12. The laws the false teachers wanted the Galatians to keep were Jewish ceremonial laws. They failed to consider what Christ has done as enough for salvation. Our faith needs to be in Christ's sacrifice, not our own ability to do what was required of the Jews in OT ceremonial law.

13. Under the law we are imprisoned in our own sin because we cannot achieve righteousness through the law. With Christ (and even the promise of Him as Messiah in the OT), came justification through faith for those who believe. We must not work for salvation but accept it as a gift of faith.

14. The OT believers had less light (looking back we can see much that was still a mystery to them) than we do. They were bound (in captivity) to a law that no one could keep perfectly but it was also a foreshadowing of Christ. God revealed Christ and His shed blood for the covering of our sin in His own timing.

15. As our "schoolmaster" the law teaches what we are not capable of keeping. We needed a new and different way to lead us to eternal life. As children need a schoolmaster to move them a long, we need a schoolmaster so we can grow and mature by turning to faith and away from the wrath of God.

16. God's Law was breathed out from God and good for teaching, reproof, correction, and training in righteousness so that Christians may be complete and equipped for every good work.

17. Though Christ does the work of salvation and faith is a gift of God, He puts on us the robe of righteousness. It is our work to keep it "renewed in knowledge" as God gives us opportunities for renewal. It seems that as we continue to "put on the new" and take whatever opportunities God provides to grow in faith and knowledge (sermons, Bible studies, Sunday School, fellowship and iron sharpening iron relationships), we become more like Christ (never fully achieving that goal).

18. The Galatians (and anyone else) did not have to keep all of the Jewish Law in order to be justified by faith in the Lord Jesus Christ.

19. Anyone (Jew, Greek, Slave, free, male, female) with faith in Jesus Christ because Abraham was counted righteous because of his faith.

Outside the Box:
Many people that Paul was writing to wanted to take the promise of Abraham as being for the Jews only when God has promised salvation by faith to anyone who believes from early in history. He fulfilled that promise in Christ. In the book of Romans, Paul teaches that Israel is the Church of Jesus Christ.

Galatians 4 Answers

Galatians 4:1-5

1. Though we are elect before the foundations of the world, God reveals Himself and our inheritance to each one of us when He wills it.
Though we experience God's gifts on earth, our inheritance and adoption will be realized to a greater extent in heaven. We wait with hope.
(Hebrews 9:15, 1 Peter 1:4)

2. "The elementary principles of the world" do not apply to the spiritual realm or offer freedom. They were outward symbols meant to point us to the need for a change of heart but a change of heart was not necessary to adhere to them.

3. Personal

4. God had planned beforehand when that day would come that He would send His Son. It was God's long term plan, not a last minute decision to try to save those whom had been lost. John Calvin said it was the "time ordained by the providence of God."

5. He was God and He was human. Also, Jesus already existed or He could not have been sent.

6. Jesus had the same requirement to keep the law as we do – only He did it. Our redemption is possible because "He who knew no sin became sin for us." He came under the Law so He could fulfill it and substitute for us in the judgment of our sin.

7. Galatians 4:4 – Father and Son; Galatians 4:6 Spirit of Son

Galatians 4:4-12

8. Paul describes God sending Christ through a woman so that He could save us and leave us with the Holy Spirit, helping us to recognize our "Abba Father." He moves us from the position of a slave (trying to keep the Law to work our way to heaven) to that of son and heir (justified by the blood of Christ for our sin).

9. The truth confirmed is that God gives us His Holy Spirit as a seal, a sign of the inheritance to come.

10.
- John 14:26 A Helper and Teacher
- Acts 1:8 the power to witness for Christ
- Romans 5:5 God's love poured into our hearts
- Romans 15:13 hope, joy, peace
- 2 Timothy 1:14 He helps us guard the deposit (treasure) entrusted to us

11. Personal

12. A slave is not an heir. A son is more than a servant to the family; he is a rightful heir, and part of the family.

13. A. He specifically names the observance of days and months and seasons and years as worthless principles.
B. He had already taught them that what they needed for salvation was faith in the death and resurrection of Jesus Christ as the propitiation for their sins. They are adding to what God requires. It was as if Paul had never taught them. What they had now learned went beyond what God requires and Paul had taught them.

Galatians 4:12-20 Notice the change, Paul softens his tone.

14. In 2 Timothy Paul teaches a method of entreating those who have wandered off the path. He tells them to do it with patience and teaching. This is what Paul is trying to do in this letter to the Galatians.

15. It would appear that in an earlier time the Galatians had received Paul when he was ill as if he were "as an angel of God, as Christ Jesus." Now, they have heard false teaching and he has been correcting them. He is reminding them that they have heard the truth and have rejected it. It has been said that it is like the course language we use when a child has run out into the street.

16. It is an act of love to give God's Truth because it is far more important to be right with God than not offended by a friend. (The wounds of a friend are faithful.)

17. Personal

18. The zeal that is for the praise of man will not last. Examples will vary.

19. Paul wants a faith that cares about the state of the faith of others. He wants them to give up old traditions and follow Christ because of their faith – get out of the birth canal and start living for Christ!

Galatians 4:21-31

20. Suggestions:

Slave	Free
Born according to the flesh (23)	Born through the promise (23)
Covenant of Mt. Sinai – the Law (25)	Corresponds to Jerusalem above – free (26)
Corresponds to present Jerusalem (25)	Our mother (26)
Persecuted one born of the Spirit (29)	Born according to the Spirit(29)
Cast out – will not inherit with the free	heir

21. The Law was given to Moses on Mt. Sinai so the people were subject to the law (which they grossly disobeyed with the golden calf) as the Pharisees in Jerusalem were teaching the law – and all they had added to it.

22. Some suggestions of our freedoms today:
Freedom from keeping the law to earn our salvation, comfort, redemption.
Freedom to receive the comfort of the Lord, Isaiah 52:9
Peace, joy, glorious abundance, Isaiah 66:10-14
Freedom to be free, 2 Corinthians and , John 8
Freedom from sin, Romans 6:7

23. He contrasts God's promises and Law. We are children of promise, not of the Law.

24. Just as Ishmael mocked Isaac, so those born according to the flesh will persecute those born according to the promise.

Outside the box: Read Genesis 21:8-12

From Genesis 21, God told and assured Abraham to follow Sarah's plan. He reminds Abraham that Isaac is the Son of the promise.

25. We are free from condemnation based on the Law. If we have faith, then Christ's righteousness is imputed to us based on His work, not our ability to keep the Law.

Galatians 5 Answers

Galatians 5:1-6

1. A. God's grace in sending Christ to die for our sin – to take our punishment – is how we are saved from an eternity in Hell. Christ accomplished the work on the cross, but until God gives us the ability to faithfully hear and respond to the gospel, it is not ours.

B. He warns that if they fall back to keeping the law (by being circumcised) for their justification, it will turn them away from God, and they will not escape death. It is faith, not circumcision that counts for anything.
God's grace in His provision of faith in the death and resurrection of Christ as the thing that paid the price for their (and our) sin is what saves. Expecting to be justified by the law they are severed from Christ.

2. Baptism, church membership, communion, confirmation, etc.

3. For the sake of the weaker brothers. Timothy subjected himself to circumcision for the sake of Jewish converts, still immature in the faith so as not to waste time arguing about circumcision but learning more of the Gospel of Christ.

4. These sacraments are commanded by God and we do them as a way to obey Him and receive the benefits of remembering Him and what he has done for us. These are acts of gratitude we should willingly participate in for God's glory and our good.

5. Through the Spirit, by faith.

6. It is only through our faith in Christ that we are capable of works that demonstrate real love. Our faith will produce works but love and works are not required to receive faith.

Galatians 5:7-12

7. A. He fears for their spiritual and eternal lives. It is far more important than a moment of discomfort or shame. They had already heard and acted on the truth of the gospel but as time and distance from him increased, it seemed they were falling away and may lead others astray as the leaven would continue to spread.

B. Yes. Today it may not be in a letter to a church – though it could be. A blog, a podcast – anything that many might hear or see that would put the Word of God before them and give opportunity to convict them of their sin. If we know someone personally, we must approach them 1-1 and exhort them – especially if they claim salvation.

8. A. Settle the disciples in the right view and allow the ones who are teaching falsely to take the (God given) penalty.

B. The cross of Christ puts everyone on a level playing field. ALL have sinned and need a Savior. Those who think they, or their teaching, is superior, or they are already God's chosen ones, as the Jewish Pharisees did, is put on the same level as the most sinful, most impoverished person on earth. Our sin is revealed on the Cross. People find that offensive.

C. He prays that they would emasculate themselves. It is not surprising in that Paul has already let off a lot of righteous anger about what they are doing to the people of God (and they would not be able to be circumcised!).

D. Yes. We often forget that God hates the evil doer (Psalm 5:5) and He is going to protect His flock – for His glory. Calvin points out in his commentary that "The glory of God is deserving of higher esteem than the salvation of men." He (Calvin) further suggests that when we see a flock of God and a wolf who is "seeking like Satan" whom he may devour, "shouldn't saving the church be purchased by the destruction of the wolf?" (Calvin's Commentaries, Volume XXI, page 157)

9. He allows the wolf to snatch and scatter the sheep. He flees because he doesn't care about the flock. Woe to this Shepherd at judgment.

Galatians 5:13-18

10. Through love, serve one another. Love your neighbor as yourself. NOT to bite and devour one another.

11. Answers will vary.

12. Personal

13. The Spirit is given by God to His elect. The better we know God (the more we interact with Him through His Word and prayer), His word, His sacrifice for our sins, and are "sharpened" by fellowship with others, the more we will see the work of the Spirit as He directs us to the work and relationships God has ordained for each one of His children.

14. A. That we are no longer under the law for our salvation.

B. Because, apparently, the false teachers were adding the law back into the work Christ had done on the cross. Paul was saying they could be done with this whole mess! They would be able to discuss Godly doctrine if they would walk by the Spirit.

Galatians 5:19-26

15. A. Personal

    B. Personal

16. Personal

17. Outside the Box: Answers will vary

18. Answers will vary.

Galatians 6 Answers

Galatians 6:1-5

1. You may come up with others:

- Humility
- Gentle words
- Love for a brother or sister
- Biblical knowledge (sound doctrine of what sin is)
- High view of God and His sovereignty
- Obedience
- Forgiving and being able to take it as well as give it (part of humility)

2. We are watching for the influence of the sin of others and our response to the conviction of the Holy Spirit about our own sin.

Outside the Box: Suggestions:
Pray for the Lord to reveal our own sin – get the log out of our own eye (Matthew 7:3)
Pray for the right words and truthful words (don't exaggerate) – Proverbs 12:18
Pray for humility and gentleness, unity – Proverbs 16:23; Ephesians 4:2-3

3. A. (Matthew 22:37-40) And he said to him, "You shall love the Lord your God with all your heart and with all your soul and with all your mind. This is the great and first commandment. And a second is like it: You shall love your neighbor as yourself. On these two commandments depend all the Law and the Prophets."
Loving our neighbors because we love Christ.

B. When we "restore a brother" we may have to walk through the consequences of sin with them. This means speaking the truth in love to them and being willing to help relieve whatever burden we can – especially the burden of sin that they will judged for if not saved.

Galatians 6:3-4

Personal

4. We will each be responsible before God for our own works – good or evil.
• God's rewarding each one according to his ways and according to the fruit of his deeds (Jeremiah 32:18-19)
• Behold, all souls are mine; the soul of the father as well as the soul of the son is mine: the soul who sins shall die. (Ezekiel 18:4)

• For the Son of Man is going to come with his angels in the glory of his Father, and then he will repay each person according to what he has done. (Matthew 16:27)
• For we must all appear before the judgment seat of Christ, so that each one may receive what is due for what he has done in the body, whether good or evil. (2 Corinthians 5:10)

Galatians 6:6-10

5. Paul was teaching the Christians that those who serve the Lord with preaching/teaching should have their basic needs met.

6.
• Preach the Word, be ready in season and out, reprove, rebuke, and exhort, with complete patience and teaching. 2 Timothy 4:2
• Teach the whole counsel of God Acts 20:27
• Not that we lord it over your faith, but we work with you for your joy, for you stand firm in your faith. 2 Corinthians 1:24
• and to bring to light for everyone what is the plan of the mystery hidden for ages in God, who created all things, Ephesians 3:9

7. A. Personal

B. Answers will vary.

8. Simply put, when we do almost anything it will either be to please the desires of our flesh (sowing to the flesh) or to honor God (sowing to the Spirit). When we know that what we are doing is against God's law – we are sowing to the flesh. When we do what we know keeps God's law and honors Him – then we are sowing to the Spirit.

9. He is teaching the Christians not to give up on doing the work of the Lord. It is as if he is warning us that we will not see immediate fruit of our labors but that if we are patient and keep going, we will be rewarded for our patience and perseverance – especially with those who are in the family of God. He prioritizes His faithful people.

10. To remind us that we are brothers and sisters, heirs with Christ, to be treated as family.

11. Answers may vary. Some suggestions:
6:1 mercy, love for all
6:5 justice
6:6 generous Provider
6:7 omniscient, generous
6:8 promise keeper, provider of salvation
6:9 Rewarder
6:10 calls for His own (faithful or loyal)

Galatians 6:11-18

12. Paul describes the behavior of men who are so concerned for their own ambitions and comfort (so they won't be persecuted) that they do not concern themselves with the truth or what will edify others. They want the Galatian Christians circumcised so they can get "credit" for their faith and be exalted by men.

13. Some suggestions from Albert Barnes, "Notes on the Bible":
• The love of God for His people in creating plan for the forgiveness of sin
• The love of Christ in His willingness to die in order to save us from eternal damnation
• The innocent died for the guilty
• The honor shown to God's Law by Christ's dying to fulfill the Law
• The reconciliation of God and man that could not be accomplished any other way
• Through the cross we become alive to Christ and dead to the world
• It's the beginning of the support and consolation which comes through the cross to sustain us in trials
• It procures for us admission into heaven

14. To crucify the world is to treat it with contempt or disdain, to no longer want what it offers, but to look to what Christ offers. The world and its temptations no longer rule us, Christ in us rules us.

15. We are spiritually new. When the love of God rules in our inner being our old mindset, worldview, and suppositions change as if we are completely new creatures. We are given new hearts (Ezekiel 36:26).

16. God's children, Abraham's offspring (Galatians 3:29); children of the promise of God (Romans 9) not necessarily those of Israel or Abraham's direct descendants, a man of the Spirit as a matter of the heart (Romans 2). These are today's born again believers in Jesus Christ.

17.
A. That they are not to listen to false teachers. He seems to say, "Stop this nonsense, I have more important things to do and you can see the truth of what I have said by the way my work has been legitimized by all the hindrances I have overcome. I have the scars to prove it!"
He wants no more hindrances to the work that God has called him to do for the sake of Christ.

B. We all have work to do. When we listen to teachers, and do not bother to check what they say with scriptures, we are led off the path that the Lord has for us to take. We allow these hindrances for too long and then face obstacles to the work God wants us to accomplish for His name's sake and the good of His people.

End Notes:

[i] Calvin's Commentaries, Volume XXI, Galatians, Ephesians, Philippians, Colossians, 1 & 2 Thessalonians, 1 & 2 Timothy, Titus, Philemon, 2003 Baker Books, Grand Rapids, Michigan. Page 79

[ii] Ibid., page 102.

[iii] Ibid.,, page 102

[iv] Calvin's Commentaries, Volume XXI, Galatians, Ephesians, Philippians, Colossians, 1 & 2 Thessalonians, 1 & 2 Timothy, Titus, Philemon, 2003 Baker Books, Grand Rapids, Michigan 49516-6287. Page 114

[v] E-Sword, Matthew Henry's Commentary on the Whole Bible, Thomas Nelson Publishers, Nashville, Tennessee, 2006. Galatians 4:1-3

[vi] Calvin's Commentaries, Volume XXI, Galatians, Ephesians, Philippians, Colossians, 1 & 2 Thessalonians, 1 & 2 Timothy, Titus, Philemon, 2003 Baker Book, Grand Rapids, Michigan. Pages 126-12

[vii] Ibid., page 140.

[viii] Ibid., page 142.

[ix] Calvin's Commentaries, Volume XXI, Galatians, Ephesians, Philippians, Colossians, 1 & 2 Thessalonians, 1 & 2 Timothy, Titus, Philemon, 2003 Baker Books, Grand Rapids, Michigan. Page 147

[x] Ibid., page 147.

[xi] Ibid., pages 149-150

[xii] Calvin's Commentaries, Volume XXI, Galatians, Ephesians, Philippians, Colossians, 1 & 2 Thessalonians, 1 & 2 Timothy, Titus, Philemon, 2003 Baker Books, Grand Rapids, Michigan 49516-6287. Page 176

[xiii] Ibid., pages 185-186

Made in the USA
Middletown, DE
01 February 2019